DOUBLE YOUR PROFIT REDUCE YOUR HASSLES

Transform your Medical Dealership to a **Money Making Machine**

DOUBLE YOUR PROFIT REDUCE YOUR HASSLES

Transform your Medical Dealership to a **Money Making Machine**

Rajesh Kanodia

Worldwide Published by
Pendown Press

PENDOWN PRESS LLP

An ISO 9001 & ISO 14001 Certified Co.,

Regd. Office: 3767A, Kanhaiya Nagar,

Tri Nagar, Delhi-110035

Ph.: 8130886000, 9650072927

E-mail: info@pendownpress.com

Branch Office: 1A/2A, 20, Hari Sadan, Ansari Road,

Daryaganj, New Delhi-110002

Ph.: 011-45794768

Website: PendownPress.com

Edition: 2024

Price: ₹ 399

ISBN: 978-93-6338-981-6

Layout and Cover Designed by Pendown Graphics Team
Printed and Bound in India by Thomson Press India Ltd.

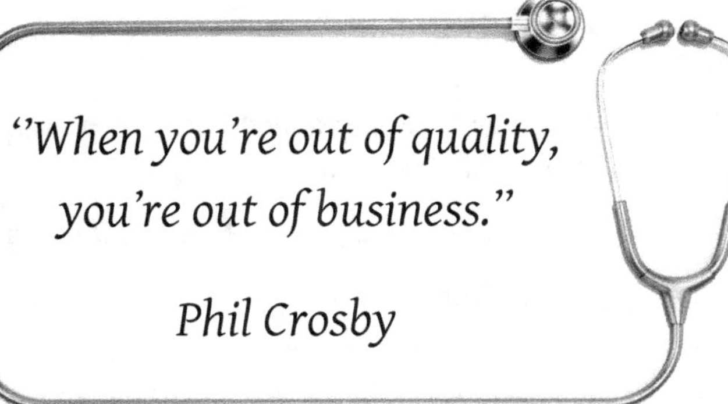

"When you're out of quality,
you're out of business."

Phil Crosby

CONTENTS

Acknowledgements

I extend my heartfelt gratitude to the individuals whose unwavering support, encouragement, and guidance have been instrumental in the creation of this book:

I am deeply indebted to my mentor, my Guru, Akshar Yadav, whose motivation and guidance inspired me to embark on this writing journey. I also extend my sincerest thanks to my captain, Pankaj Bengani, for his invaluable advice and expertise. Their insights have shaped this book in profound ways, and I am honored to have learned from their wisdom.

To my beloved wife Shreya and my daughters, Meenakshi and Aparna, I am profoundly grateful for your boundless love, patience, and understanding throughout the writing process. Meenakshi's skillful design of the cover page and Aparna's meticulous editing have enhanced the quality of this book. Your unwavering support has been my anchor, and I am endlessly thankful for your belief in me.

A special thank you to Dr. (Prof.) Sanjay Rajpal, Naresh Poddar, and others, whose constant encouragement and words of wisdom have fueled my determination to see this project through. Your friendship has been a source of inspiration and motivation, and I am grateful for the laughter and camaraderie we've shared along the way.

Lastly, to all those whose names may not be mentioned but whose contributions, support, and encouragement have left an indelible mark on my journey—thank you. Your presence, whether felt directly or indirectly, has enriched this endeavor beyond measure.

About The Author

Greetings,

I am **Rajesh Kanodia**, a passionate advocate for healthcare excellence and a Pharmacy Graduate with over three decades of dedicated service to the healthcare sector. As the Founder and Director of Sara Healthcare Private Limited, I have spearheaded a mission to revolutionize healthcare accessibility in India.

My journey began over 30 years ago, driven by a relentless commitment to providing top-quality healthcare products at affordable prices, with the ultimate goal of fostering a healthier nation. What started as a vision has evolved into Sara Healthcare Private Limited, now recognized as the fastest-growing company in the healthcare industry.

Throughout our journey, we have garnered prestigious awards and accolades, including recognition from esteemed institutions such as the Indian Medical Association (Ayush). Our dedication to innovation and unparalleled service has set new benchmarks in the healthcare landscape in India.

At the helm of Sara Healthcare, I have led pioneering initiatives that have reshaped the healthcare landscape of India. From importing high-quality medical devices to pioneering domestic manufacturing, our endeavors have propelled us to the forefront of the industry. Notably, we secured one of the first manufacturing licenses issued by the Government of India under the Medical Device Rules, a testament to our unwavering commitment to excellence and compliance.

But beyond the accolades and achievements lies a deeper purpose — a dedication to making a meaningful difference in the lives of millions. Our journey is not merely about business success; it is about empowering individuals and communities through access to superior healthcare solutions.

I am immensely proud of the journey thus far, but our mission is far from over. As we continue to innovate, collaborate, and advocate for a healthier tomorrow, I invite you to join us in our quest to redefine healthcare in India and beyond.

Together, let us pave the way towards a healthier, happier future.

Warm regards,

Rajesh Kanodia
Founder and Director, Sara Healthcare Pvt. Ltd.

Why This Book?

Dear Reader,

After three decades in the healthcare industry, I've encountered numerous challenges, made my fair share of mistakes, and perhaps, wasted more than a few resources along the way.

These experiences fuelled my desire to pen this book—to share the lessons learned, save you from repeating my missteps, and spare you the loss of time and money you might otherwise face.

While personal meetings offer a platform for sharing insights, the entire spectrum of my experiences and learnings can't be fully conveyed in those interactions alone.

Also due to time & logistics constraints, it's impossible to reach the large number of people I want to benefit from my learnings. Hence, this book offers my wisdom & expertise—as a collection of all the valuable practical lessons drawn from navigating the field of healthcare business for 3 decades.

My intent is simple and unwavering: to extend a helping hand, to empower you with knowledge that could potentially make a significant difference in your journey. I am sure that within these pages, you'll find not just guidance, but also inspiration to navigate the complexities of the healthcare industry with greater foresight and confidence.

With warm regards,

Rajesh Kanodia

The essence of quality is building the customer's trust and loyalty

Narayana Murthy

CHAPTER-1

INTRODUCTION

INTRODUCTION

Medical devices are like superheroes in healthcare—they help doctors diagnose illnesses, treat patients, and keep an eye on their health.

In India, these gadgets are crucial because they make healthcare accessible to people, even in far-off places.

Think of X-ray machines, ultrasound scanners, blood pressure monitors and thermometers — all examples of medical devices that doctors use to help patients. When someone needs surgery, special tools like surgical lasers and robotic systems help doctors work their magic safely and precisely.

For people with chronic conditions like diabetes or asthmatic bronchitis, medical devices are lifesavers. Devices like glucometers and nebulizers help them keep track of their health and manage their conditions better.

But it's not just about treating diseases—medical devices also help people who need long-term care or rehabilitation. Wheelchairs, prosthetic limbs, and hearing aids are common examples of devices that make life easier for people with disabilities or long-term health issues.

And let's not forget about the new gadgets that are changing the healthcare landscape radically, like smart watches that monitor your heart rate or apps that let you talk to a doctor from the comfort of your own home. These innovations are making healthcare smarter, more personalized, and more accessible for everyone.

To take this a step further and show you the importance and impact of medical devices, let me share some more ways that these unsung heroes are making the world a better place indeed.

- **Portable Diagnostic Devices:** Devices like portable ultrasound machines and handheld ECG monitors are revolutionizing healthcare in remote areas. These tools allow healthcare professionals to conduct essential diagnostics without needing to transport patients to distant medical facilities.

- **Implantable Devices:** Pacemakers, and insulin pumps are great examples of implantable medical devices that come as rays of hope to improve the quality of life for patients with heart conditions or diabetes. These devices continuously monitor and manage health conditions, providing critical interventions when needed.

- **Telemedicine Equipment:** With the rise of telemedicine during and post the pandemic, devices like high-resolution cameras and digital stethoscopes are enabling remote consultations smoothly and effectively. This is particularly beneficial in rural India, where access to specialists and modes of medical transportation can be limited.

- **Advanced Surgical Tools:** Cutting-edge innovations like laparoscopic instruments and robotic surgery systems are enhancing surgical precision and reducing recovery times. These technologies enable minimally invasive procedures, leading to less pain & distress, fewer complications and shorter hospital stays.

- **Monitoring Systems:** Continuous glucose monitors (CGMs) for diabetes management and wearable cardiac monitors for patients with heart conditions provide real-time data to both patients and healthcare providers, allowing for better treatment plans and immediate intervention if needed.

- **Therapeutic Devices:** Equipment like dialysis machines for kidney failure patients and CPAP machines for those with sleep apnea are vital for managing chronic conditions. These devices not only improve patients' quality of life but also extend their life expectancy.

- **Innovative Consumer Health Devices:** Fitness trackers and health monitoring apps are encouraging and empowering regular people to take charge of their health. These devices track physical activity, sleep patterns, and vital signs, providing valuable data that can be shared with healthcare providers for a better health assessment.

In a nutshell, medical devices are like the unsung heroes of healthcare—they help doctors save lives, improve quality of life, and make healthcare more convenient for everyone. From essential diagnostic tools to advanced therapeutic equipment, these devices are integral to modern medicine, making healthcare more efficient, effective, and accessible across the globe.

CHAPTER-2

UNDERSTANDING THE IMPORTANCE OF QUALITY IN MEDICAL DEVICES

UNDERSTANDING THE IMPORTANCE OF QUALITY IN MEDICAL DEVICES

Quality in medical devices consists of several key attributes that ensure their safety, reliability, and effectiveness in diagnosing, treating, and monitoring health conditions.

Here's a breakdown of what constitutes quality in medical devices:

1. **Safety:** Safety is paramount in medical devices. Safety comes from quality. A quality device should be designed, manufactured, and used in a way that minimizes risks to patients, operators, and bystanders. The manufacturer should ensure that it complies with all the regulatory standards and has undergone rigorous testing so that it poses no undue harm.

2. **Reliability:** Reliability refers to the consistent performance of a medical device over time and under various conditions. A quality device should function reliably without malfunctioning or producing inaccurate results. It should maintain its performance throughout its intended lifespan.

3. **Accuracy:** Accuracy is critical for all medical devices that measure physiological parameters or deliver therapeutic interventions. A quality device should provide precise and consistent measurements or treatments that align with established clinical standards. Any margin of error should be minimal and well-documented.

4. **Durability:** Medical devices are subject to frequent use and sometimes harsh environmental conditions. A quality device should be durable enough to withstand regular wear and tear without compromising its functionality or safety. It should be

built from high-quality materials and undergo robust testing for durability.

5. **Ease of Use:** Medical devices should be user-friendly, allowing healthcare professionals to operate them efficiently and effectively. A quality device should have clear instructions for use, ergonomic design features, and minimal setup or calibration requirements. Training requirements for users should also be manageable.

6. **Compatibility:** Quality medical devices should integrate seamlessly with existing healthcare systems and workflows. They should be compatible with other devices, software platforms, and electronic health records to facilitate data exchange and interoperability. Compatibility ensures smooth integration into clinical practice and enhances overall efficiency.

7. **Regulatory Compliance:** Compliance with regulatory requirements is essential for ensuring the safety and effectiveness of medical devices. A quality device should meet all applicable regulatory standards and undergo thorough regulatory review processes before being marketed or distributed. This includes compliance with standards such as ISO 13485 for quality management systems and adherence to regulations set forth by regulatory bodies like the FDA or CE Marking.

By upholding these attributes of quality, medical device manufacturers can instill confidence in healthcare providers and patients, ultimately improving patient outcomes and advancing the quality of healthcare delivery.

The impact of quality medical devices on patient outcomes and healthcare provider satisfaction cannot be emphasized enough.

In the section below, I elaborate on how quality devices contribute positively to both:

1. **Improved Patient Outcomes**

   - **Accuracy and Reliability:** Quality medical devices provide accurate and reliable measurements, diagnoses, and treatments, leading to more precise medical interventions and better patient outcomes.

   - **Timely Intervention:** With reliable data from quality devices, healthcare providers can identify and address health issues promptly, preventing complications and improving treatment efficacy.

   - **Reduced Errors:** Quality devices minimize the risk of errors, such as misdiagnoses or incorrect dosages, which can lead to adverse events or treatment failures. This ultimately results in safer patient care and better health outcomes.

   - **Enhanced Monitoring:** Advanced monitoring capabilities in quality devices allow healthcare providers to closely monitor patients' vital signs and response to treatment, enabling early detection of any deviations and timely adjustments to the care plan.

2. **Increased Healthcare Provider Satisfaction**

   - **Efficiency and Effectiveness:** Quality medical devices streamline healthcare workflows, making tasks easier and more efficient for healthcare providers. This allows them to focus more on patient care with a free mind as they do not need to worry about device shortcomings or troubleshooting.

   - **Confidence and Trust:** Healthcare providers rely on quality devices to deliver accurate information and support their clinical diagnoses and decisions. Using reliable equipment enhances their confidence in their ability to deliver high-quality care.

- **Enhanced User Experience:** User-friendly interfaces and features in quality devices contribute to a positive user experience for healthcare professionals. Easy-to-use devices reduce frustration and allow them to perform their duties with greater ease and satisfaction.

- **Professional Reputation:** Using quality devices is essential not only for better delivery, diagnoses and decision-making, but it also impacts a healthcare professional's reputation hugely.

Healthcare professionals who use quality devices are perceived as competent and dedicated to patient safety and well-being. This enhances their professional reputation and satisfaction, leading to greater job fulfillment and retention.

Overall, quality medical devices play a vital role in ensuring positive patient outcomes and enhancing job satisfaction and fulfillment in healthcare professionals.

By investing in quality devices, healthcare facilities can improve the quality of care, increase patient satisfaction, and create a more supportive and rewarding work environment for their staff.

NOTES

Date ...... /..... /..........

CHAPTER-3

RISKS ASSOCIATED WITH CHEAP MEDICAL DEVICES

RISKS ASSOCIATED WITH CHEAP MEDICAL DEVICES

Using low-quality or cheap medical devices can pose significant dangers to patients, healthcare providers, and healthcare facilities. It would not be wrong to say that cheap, low-quality devices though apparently attractively priced can pose serious risks to patients and end up damaging the reputation of the associated healthcare professionals and health care facilities.

Here are some potential dangers associated with such devices:

1. **Inaccurate Readings or Measurements:** Low-quality medical devices may provide inaccurate or unreliable readings, leading to misdiagnoses, incorrect treatment decisions, or ineffective patient monitoring. **This can result in delayed interventions, escalation of health conditions, or even patient harm & fatality.**

2. **Safety Hazards:** Cheaply made medical devices may lack essential safety features or fail to meet regulatory standards, increasing the risk of adverse events, injuries, or infections. Malfunctions or defects in these devices can pose serious safety hazards to patients undergoing diagnostic procedures, treatments, or surgeries.

3. **Poor Performance and Durability:** Low-quality devices are more prone to malfunction, breakdown, or premature failure, compromising their performance and durability.

   This can disrupt healthcare services, increase maintenance costs, and necessitate frequent replacements, leading to operational inefficiencies and financial burdens for healthcare facilities.

4. **Compromised Infection Control:** Substandard medical devices may not adhere to strict infection control standards or undergo proper sterilization procedures, posing a risk of cross-contamination and healthcare-associated infections (HAIs). Inadequate sterilization or cleaning protocols can contribute to the spread of infectious diseases among patients and healthcare workers.

5. **Legal and Regulatory Compliance Issues:** Using cheap medical devices that do not meet regulatory requirements or quality standards can expose healthcare providers and facilities to legal liability, fines, or sanctions.

   Non-compliance with regulatory guidelines may result in enforcement actions, reputational damage, and loss of trust among patients and stakeholders.

6. **Negative Impact on Patient Experience:** Patients may experience discomfort, anxiety, or dissatisfaction when subjected to low-quality medical devices that are unreliable, uncomfortable, or difficult to use. Poor patient experiences can undermine trust in healthcare providers, reduce patient satisfaction, and lead to negative reviews or complaints.

7. **Financial Costs and Wastage:** While cheap medical devices may seem cost-effective initially, **they can incur higher long-term costs due to frequent repairs, replacements, or adverse outcomes.** Investing in quality devices may result in upfront savings and better value for money over time by reducing the need for costly interventions or corrective measures.

In summary, the use of low-quality or cheap medical devices can have serious implications for patient safety, healthcare quality, and financial sustainability.

Healthcare providers and facilities must prioritize the procurement of high-quality devices that meet stringent standards and adhere to regulatory requirements to ensure the delivery of safe, effective, and reliable care to patients.

Real-Life Consequences of Substandard Devices

A Case Study

The scenario: A clinic purchases low-cost thermometers from an unverified supplier.

The Consequences

- **Substandard Devices:** The thermometers consistently provide inaccurate temperature readings, leading to misdiagnoses of fever-related illnesses. Patients are either unnecessarily treated for non-existent fevers or fail to receive treatment for actual infections.

The Impact

- **Reputational Damage:** The clinic's reputation suffers as patients become dissatisfied with the quality of care. Negative online reviews and word-of-mouth spread, resulting in a loss of trust and potential legal liabilities for the clinic.

"I am compelled to express my gratitude to Sara Healthcare Pvt Ltd for providing exemplary surgical products that have significantly elevated the standard of care in my medical practice.

I, wholeheartedly, recommend Sara Healthcare Pvt Ltd to my colleagues for their unwavering dedication to excellence in advancing the field of healthcare."

Dr. Manju Rajpal
Leading Family Physician

Using Cheap vs. Quality Medical Devices: A Comparison

Scenario 1: A hospital purchases inexpensive blood pressure monitors from a lesser-known manufacturer to cut costs.

- **Cheap Medical Devices:** The blood pressure monitors consistently provide inaccurate readings, leading to misdiagnoses & inappropriate treatment decisions. Patients experience complications due to undetected hypertension or incorrect medication dosages.

Scenario 2: Another hospital chooses to invest in a quality product even though it comes at a slightly higher cost.

The Impact

- Quality Medical Devices: In contrast, another hospital invests in high-quality blood pressure monitors from a reputable manufacturer. The monitors provide accurate readings, enabling healthcare providers to make informed treatment decisions. Patients receive timely interventions, leading to improved outcomes and higher satisfaction rates.

"As a practicing doctor, I want to express my sincere appreciation to **Sara Healthcare Pvt Ltd** for providing exceptional surgical products that have significantly enhanced the precision and success of my procedures.

I sincerely endorse Sara Healthcare Pvt. Ltd. products to my fellow medical professionals. Thank you for consistently delivering products that contribute to the success of surgical interventions."

Dr. Vrinda Khemani Kela

MS (Obs & Gynae)

NOTES

Date ...... /..... /..........

CHAPTER-4

FACTORS TO CONSIDER WHEN SELECTING MEDICAL DEVICES

FACTORS TO CONSIDER WHEN SELECTING MEDICAL DEVICES

As discussed and reiterated at several places in this book, choosing the right medical devices is essential for distributors for several key reasons such as patient safety and outcomes, regulatory compliance, the distributor's own reputation and trust, minimized liability, cost-effectiveness, market competitiveness, patient satisfaction and trust in healthcare.

Based on my years of experience & expertise, here's a comprehensive guide for distributors detailing the factors to consider when choosing medical devices:

1. **Clinical Needs Assessment**

   - Understand the specific clinical needs and requirements of healthcare providers and facilities to ensure that the chosen medical devices align with their patient population, specialty areas, and treatment protocols.

2. **Quality and Safety**

   - Prioritize medical devices from reputable manufacturers with a proven track record of quality, safety, and regulatory compliance.

   - Verify that devices meet relevant industry standards, adhere to regulatory requirements (e.g., FDA approval, CE marking), and have undergone rigorous testing and certification processes.

3. **Reliability and Durability**

   - Evaluate the reliability and durability of medical devices, considering factors such as build quality, materials used, and resistance to wear and tear.

- Choose devices that can withstand the demands of clinical use, including frequent sterilization, cleaning, and disinfection procedures.

4. Accuracy and Performance

- Assess the accuracy, precision, and performance characteristics of medical devices, ensuring they provide reliable and consistent results.

- Look for devices with validated measurement capabilities, low error rates, and proven clinical efficacy in relevant applications.

5. Ease of Use and User Experience

- Consider the usability and user experience of medical devices, including intuitive interfaces, ergonomic design features, and clear instructions for operation.

- Choose devices that require minimal training for healthcare staff and facilitate efficient workflow integration in clinical settings.

6. Compatibility and Interoperability

- Ensure that medical devices are compatible with existing healthcare infrastructure, electronic health records (EHR) systems, and interoperability standards.

- Select devices that support seamless data exchange, integration, and connectivity with other healthcare technologies to enhance care coordination and information sharing.

7. Service and Support

- Evaluate the availability and responsiveness of technical support, maintenance services, and after-sales support provided by the manufacturer or authorized distributors.

- Consider factors such as warranty coverage, service contracts, and availability of spare parts to support ongoing device maintenance and troubleshooting needs.

8. Cost and Value

- Consider the total cost of ownership, including upfront purchase costs, ongoing maintenance expenses, and potential savings from improved efficiency or patient outcomes.

- Balance cost considerations with the value proposition offered by medical devices, prioritizing investments that deliver long-term benefits and return on investment and not merely short-term cost savings..

9. Regulatory Compliance and Documentation

- Ensure that medical devices comply with relevant regulatory requirements and documentation standards, including labeling, instructions for use, and risk management documentation.

- Verify the availability of regulatory documentation, such as certificates of compliance, regulatory filings, and post-market surveillance reports, to demonstrate regulatory compliance and facilitate regulatory audits or inspections.

By considering these comprehensive factors, you as distributors can make informed decisions when selecting medical devices, ultimately contributing to improved patient care, healthcare outcomes, and provider satisfaction.

NOTES

Date ...... /..... /..........

NOTES

Date ...... /..... /.........

CHAPTER-5

THE LONG-TERM BENEFITS OF INVESTING IN QUALITY

THE LONG-TERM BENEFITS OF INVESTING IN QUALITY

Investing in quality medical devices offers numerous advantages for both distributors and end-users.

In this chapter, let's explore and understand these benefits in detail:

Advantages for Distributors

1. **Enhanced Reputation and Trust:** Distributors who offer high-quality medical devices from reputable manufacturers build a positive reputation in the healthcare industry. This fosters trust among healthcare providers, leading to increased customer loyalty and repeat business.

2. **Competitive Advantage:** Quality medical devices differentiate distributors from competitors who may offer cheaper, inferior alternatives. By prioritizing quality over price, distributors can position themselves as trusted partners in delivering safe and effective healthcare solutions.

3. **Long-Term Partnerships:** Distributors who provide quality medical devices establish long-term partnerships with healthcare facilities and providers. These partnerships are built on reliability, consistency, and a shared commitment to patient safety and well-being.

4. **Reduced Liability and Risk:** Offering high-quality medical devices reduces the risk of liability associated with distributing substandard or faulty products. By adhering to regulatory standards and industry best practices, distributors mitigate legal and financial risks associated with product recalls, lawsuits, or regulatory penalties.

5. **Streamlined Operations:** Quality medical devices are less likely to malfunction or require frequent repairs, resulting in fewer disruptions to operations and reduced administrative burden. This allows distributors to focus on core business activities and provide better support to customers.

Advantages for End-Users (Healthcare Providers & Patients)

1. **Improved Patient Outcomes:** Quality medical devices contribute to better patient outcomes by providing accurate diagnostics, precise treatments, and reliable monitoring. This leads to more effective healthcare interventions, reduced complications, and faster recovery times for patients.

2. **Enhanced Safety and Reliability:** End-users benefit from the safety and reliability of quality medical devices, which undergo rigorous testing and adhere to stringent quality standards. This minimizes the risk of errors, adverse events, and patient harm, instilling confidence in healthcare providers and patients alike.

3. **Long-Term Cost Savings:** While quality medical devices may have higher upfront costs, they offer long-term cost savings by reducing the need for repairs, replacements, or corrective measures. Investing in quality devices lowers total cost of ownership over time and improves return on investment for healthcare facilities.

4. **Positive Patient Experience:** Patients receive better care and experience greater satisfaction when treated with quality medical devices. User-friendly interfaces, comfortable designs, and accurate results enhance the patient experience and promote trust in the healthcare provider.

5. **High-Quality Care Delivery:** Quality medical devices enable healthcare providers to deliver high-quality care that meets

or exceeds industry standards. By using reliable tools and technologies, providers can focus on delivering personalized, evidence-based care that improves patient outcomes and enhances overall healthcare delivery.

In summary, investing in quality medical devices benefits distributors by enhancing reputation, reducing risk, and fostering long-term partnerships. End-users benefit from improved patient outcomes, enhanced safety, cost savings, and a superior healthcare experience. Ultimately, prioritizing quality in medical device procurement benefits the entire healthcare ecosystem by promoting safety, efficiency, and excellence in patient care.

Success Stories of Distributors Prioritizing Quality: Real Client Experiences

The scenario: A distributor specializing in surgical instruments partners with top manufacturers known for their quality and reliability.

The Impact

- **Success Story:** By prioritizing quality over price, the distributor establishes a reputation for reliability and trustworthiness among healthcare providers. Surgeons praise the superior performance and durability of the surgical instruments, resulting in increased demand and market share for the distributor.

- **Positive Outcomes:** Healthcare facilities experience fewer instrument malfunctions or failures during surgeries, leading to smoother procedures and reduced risk of complications. Patients benefit from safer surgeries, faster recovery times, and overall better outcomes.

 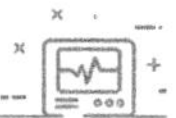

"We have been associated with **Sara Healthcare Pvt Ltd** since 2007 and we are incredibly pleased with the exceptional surgical products provided by **Sara Healthcare Pvt Ltd.**

My business has grown by **5x** with the support of **Sara Healthcare Pvt Ltd.** We wholeheartedly recommend **Sara Healthcare Pvt Ltd** to any healthcare institution seeking cutting-edge and reliable surgical solutions."

Viral Nawab

Shree Vimal Agency (Ahmedabad)

"Our experience as a distributor for **Sara Healthcare Pvt Ltd** has been nothing short of exceptional.

The superior quality and reliability of their surgical products have not only satisfied our customers but have also elevated our position in the market.

We wholeheartedly endorse **Sara Healthcare Pvt Ltd** to fellow distributors seeking a reliable and innovative partner in the surgical industry.

Thank you for consistently exceeding our expectations and contributing to our mutual success."

Praveen Manchanda

Tulip Pharma (New Delhi)

NOTES

Date ...... /..... /.........

CHAPTER-6

BUILDING TRUST WITH YOUR CUSTOMERS

BUILDING TRUST WITH YOUR CUSTOMERS

Building trust with customers is essential for any distributor in the healthcare industry. Trust forms the foundation of strong relationships, fosters loyalty, and enhances reputation.

In a sector where reliability and integrity are of utmost importance, trust ensures that customers feel confident in the products and services provided, which is critical for both patient safety and business success.

By establishing trust, distributors can develop long-term partnerships, secure repeat business, and benefit from positive word-of-mouth referrals.

This not only drives customer retention and increases sales but also strengthens the distributor's market position, ultimately leading to greater profitability and sustainable growth.

Here are some strategies distributors can employ to build trust with their customers:

1. **Prioritizing Quality Products:** One of the most effective ways to build trust with customers is by prioritizing the quality of products offered.

    Distributors should partner with reputable manufacturers known for producing high-quality, reliable medical devices.

    By ensuring that the products they offer meet stringent quality standards and regulatory requirements, distributors demonstrate their commitment to delivering safe and effective solutions to customers.

2. **Establishing Transparency & Open Communication:** Transparency is key to building trust. Distributors should

maintain open and honest communication with customers regarding product specifications, pricing, and any potential limitations or risks. **Providing clear and accurate information helps to establish credibility and fosters trust** between the distributor and the customer.

3. **Providing Exceptional Customer Service and Support:** Exceptional customer service goes a long way in building trust and loyalty. Distributors should prioritize responsiveness and attentiveness to customer inquiries, concerns, and needs. By providing timely assistance and support, distributors demonstrate their commitment to customer satisfaction and build trust over time.

   This customer service should not be limited to pre-sales or during sales only, after-sales service of equipment where applicable is essential to building trust & loyalty, thus driving business & profits.

4. **Demonstrating Expertise and Knowledge:** Customers trust distributors who demonstrate expertise and knowledge in their field. **Distributors should invest in educating their sales and support teams** on the products they offer, as well as industry trends and best practices. **By providing informed guidance and recommendations, distributors position themselves as trusted advisors** to their customers and elevate themselves from yet another vendor to a preferred growth partner.

5. **Delivering Consistent Value:** Consistently delivering value to customers is essential for building trust and loyalty. Distributors should strive to offer competitive pricing, reliable product availability, and additional value-added services such as training, technical support, and product demonstrations. By consistently

meeting or exceeding customer expectations, distributors earn the trust and loyalty of their customers.

6. Highlight Manufacturer Partnerships: Showcase partnerships with reputable manufacturers known for producing high-quality, reliable medical devices. Leveraging manufacturer credibility reinforces the distributor's commitment to offering trusted products and services.

In summary, building trust with customers requires a commitment to quality, transparency, exceptional service, expertise, and consistent value delivery. By prioritizing these aspects in their interactions with customers, distributors can build strong and enduring relationships that benefit both parties in the long run.

Distributors Benefiting from Quality Products: Building Long-lasting Trust

The scenario: A distributor of medical equipment partners with renowned manufacturers known for their quality and accuracy.

- **Success Story:** The distributor focuses on educating healthcare providers about the benefits of using high-quality diagnostic equipment. Through demonstrations and training sessions, providers gain confidence in the reliability and accuracy of the products.

- **Positive Outcomes:** Healthcare facilities experience fewer diagnostic errors and faster patient throughput due to the efficiency of the equipment. Patients receive timely and accurate diagnoses, leading to improved treatment outcomes and higher satisfaction scores leading to long-term trust and repeat business.

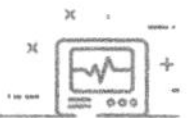

"Our partnership with **Sara Healthcare Pvt Ltd** has been exceptionally rewarding as a distributor of their surgical products.

The quality and innovation inherent in their product line have not only met but exceeded our expectations, earning the trust of our customers and contributing significantly to our business growth by 3x.

Thank you for your unwavering dedication to quality and innovation, and we look forward to a continued successful collaboration. "

Rajan Chanda
Hans Surgical Pvt Ltd (New Delhi)

"**Our experience of more than 11 years with Sara Healthcare Pvt Ltd** has been outstanding.

The quality, reliability and quantity of your surgical products have greatly enhanced the success of our medical business.

We highly recommend **Sara Healthcare Pvt Ltd** products to any healthcare facility seeking cutting-edge technology and a dedicated partner in advancing patient care."

Varun Batra
Sharnagat Prabhu Ram Medicose, Dehradun

NOTES

Date ...... /..... /..........

CHAPTER-7

ENSURING COMPLIANCE AND SAFETY STANDARDS

ENSURING COMPLIANCE AND SAFETY STANDARDS: A CRITICAL RESPONSIBILITY FOR DISTRIBUTORS

As shared & discussed in the earlier chapters, establishing trust and reliability in the healthcare industry is mandatory, as they form the foundation of successful relationships between distributors, healthcare providers, and patients.

Ensuring & adhering to all regulatory compliance standards is a huge part of being trustworthy & reliable.

It is not just a regulatory requirement—it's a moral duty.

For distributors of medical devices, this responsibility is crucial as it directly impacts patient safety, the delivery of healthcare, and the reputation of healthcare professionals and their own businesses.

Rigorously maintaining compliance with safety standards ensures that medical devices perform as intended, without causing harm to patients or users.

Regulatory bodies, usually set strict guidelines that manufacturers and distributors must follow to ensure the safety and efficacy of medical devices.

For distributors, adhering to these standards is vital for several reasons:

1. **Patient Safety:** The primary goal of any medical device is to improve patient results and experience. Ensuring compliance means that the devices distributed are safe, reliable, and effective, thus protecting patients from potential harm.

2. **Healthcare Delivery:** Compliance also guarantees that healthcare professionals have access to high-quality tools they

can trust. This reliability is essential for accurate diagnosis, effective treatment, and overall quality of treatment and care.

3. **Reputation Management:** A distributor known for delivering compliant, safe, and high-quality medical devices builds a strong reputation in the market. This reputation is invaluable, fostering trust and long-term relationships with healthcare providers and other stakeholders.

Distributors play a key role in the healthcare supply chain. Their responsibilities include:

1. **Vetting Manufacturers:** A distributor is only as good as the manufacturer they source equipment from, and must thoroughly evaluate the manufacturers they partner with to ensure they adhere to all relevant safety and compliance standards. This includes reviewing certifications, quality control processes, and past performance.

2. **Training and Education:** Distributors should provide training to healthcare professionals on the proper use of medical devices. This ensures that the devices are used correctly, minimizing the risk of errors and enhancing patient safety. They will be able to do this well if their manufacturer is knowledgeable about the equipment they are supplying & shares that knowledge with them.

3. **Staying Informed:** The regulatory landscape is constantly evolving. Distributors must stay up-to-date with changes in regulations and standards to ensure ongoing compliance. This might involve regular training, attending industry conferences, and subscribing to relevant publications.

Non-compliant medical devices can lead to severe consequences, including inaccurate diagnoses, ineffective treatments, and even patient injuries or fatalities.

By ensuring compliance, distributors help prevent these outcomes, safeguarding patient health and well-being.

Healthcare professionals rely on medical devices to provide the best possible care.

Non-compliant devices can disrupt this process, leading to mistrust, inefficiencies, and potentially harmful outcomes.

By delivering compliant and safe devices, distributors ensure that healthcare providers can perform their duties effectively, and with confidence in the tools they are using.

Distributors who consistently deliver high-quality, compliant medical devices build a reputation for reliability and integrity.

This reputation can lead to increased business opportunities, stronger partnerships, and a competitive edge in the market.

On the other hand, distributing non-compliant devices can result in legal issues, financial losses, and a damaged reputation that is difficult to recover.

Remember, financial losses are still something that you can recover from, however, if your reputation takes a hit, that is difficult to recover from.

Ensuring the compliance and safety standards of the devices & equipment you represent is a fundamental responsibility for distributors of medical devices.

It protects patients, supports healthcare professionals, and safeguards your reputation. By prioritizing compliance and safety, distributors not only fulfill their regulatory obligations but also contribute to the overall quality and reliability of healthcare delivery.

This commitment to excellence is essential for building trust and achieving long-term success in the healthcare industry.

NOTES

Date ...... /..... /..........

NOTES

Date ...... /..... /..........

CHAPTER-8

CONCLUSION: COMMITTING TO EXCELLENCE

CONCLUSION: COMMITTING TO EXCELLENCE

Summary of Key Points

Throughout this book, we've explored the critical importance of prioritizing quality in medical devices and the profound impact it has on healthcare providers, patients, and distributors alike.

Here is a ready reference summary of the key points discussed:

1. **Significance of Quality:** Quality in medical devices is non-negotiable. It ensures patient safety, reliability, and effectiveness in diagnosing, treating, and monitoring health conditions.

2. **Consequences of Substandard Devices:** Using cheap or low-quality medical devices can lead to inaccuracies, malfunctions, safety hazards, and compromised patient outcomes. Such devices pose risks to patient safety and can damage the reputation of healthcare providers and distributors.

3. **Advantages of Quality Devices:** Investing in quality medical devices offers numerous benefits, including improved patient outcomes, enhanced safety, long-term cost savings, and a competitive edge in the market.

4. **Strategies for Distributors:** Distributors can build trust and credibility by prioritizing quality in their product offerings and committing to excellence in serving their customers. This includes partnering with reputable manufacturers, ensuring regulatory compliance, providing exceptional customer service, and fostering long-term relationships with healthcare providers.

Encouragement to Prioritize Quality

As distributors, it's imperative that we prioritize quality in our product offerings and commit to excellence in serving our customers. By choosing quality medical devices over cheaper alternatives, we not only uphold the highest standards of patient care but also strengthen our reputation and credibility in the healthcare industry.

- Let's remember that our actions as distributors have a direct impact on patient safety and healthcare outcomes. By prioritizing quality, we contribute to a culture of excellence and trust within the healthcare ecosystem, ultimately benefiting healthcare providers, patients, and ourselves.

- Together, let's make a commitment to prioritize quality in everything we do and strive to be leaders in delivering safe, effective, and reliable medical devices to healthcare providers and patients around the world.

In conclusion, based on my extensive experience, I urge all ambitious business owners not to succumb to short-term thinking. Instead, cultivate a long-term vision for your enterprise, anchored in your core values and ethics. By prioritizing customer satisfaction, trust, and relationship-building, you pave the way for sustainable growth and success.

Refuse to compromise your reputation by associating with unethical companies solely for the sake of cheaper prices. Such short-sighted decisions may lead to being labeled as a cheap supplier, undermining your future prospects in the market.

This brief insight into my journey underscores the importance of adopting a strategic approach to business. Even small steps, guided by integrity and a commitment to excellence, can yield transformative results.

For those seeking further guidance and detailed insights into navigating this journey, I invite you to connect with me directly to schedule a one-on-one consultation via **e-mail at rajesh@ sarahealthcare.com.**

Remember, it's not just about reaching your goals—it's about how you get there and the legacy you leave behind. Choose wisely, invest in trust, and watch your business thrive.

○ ○ ○ ○

NOTES

Date ...... /..... /..........

NOTES

Date ...... /..... /.........

www.ingramcontent.com/pod-product-compliance
Lightning Source LLC
Chambersburg PA
CBHW061640130726
47996CB00003B/1395